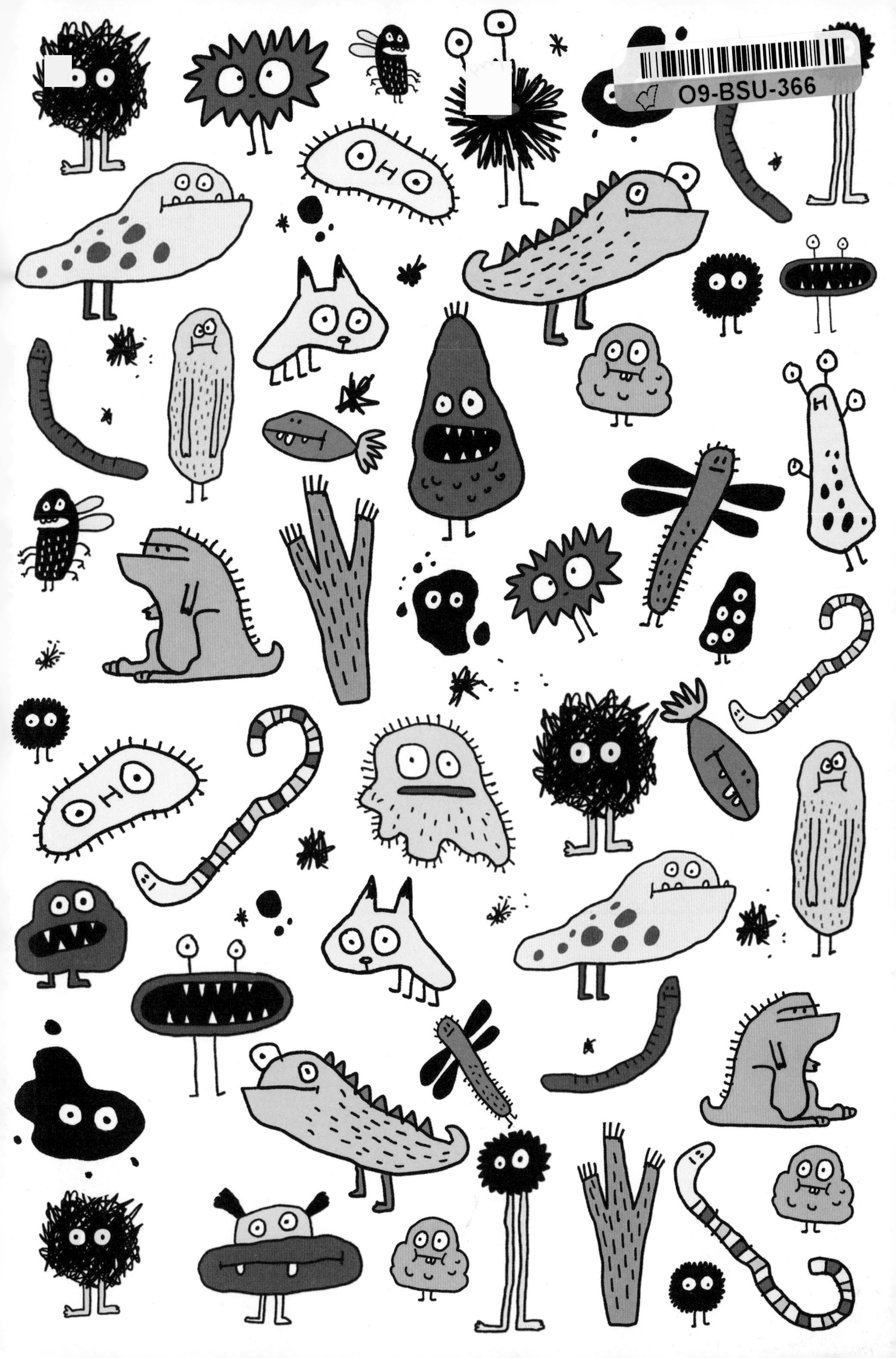

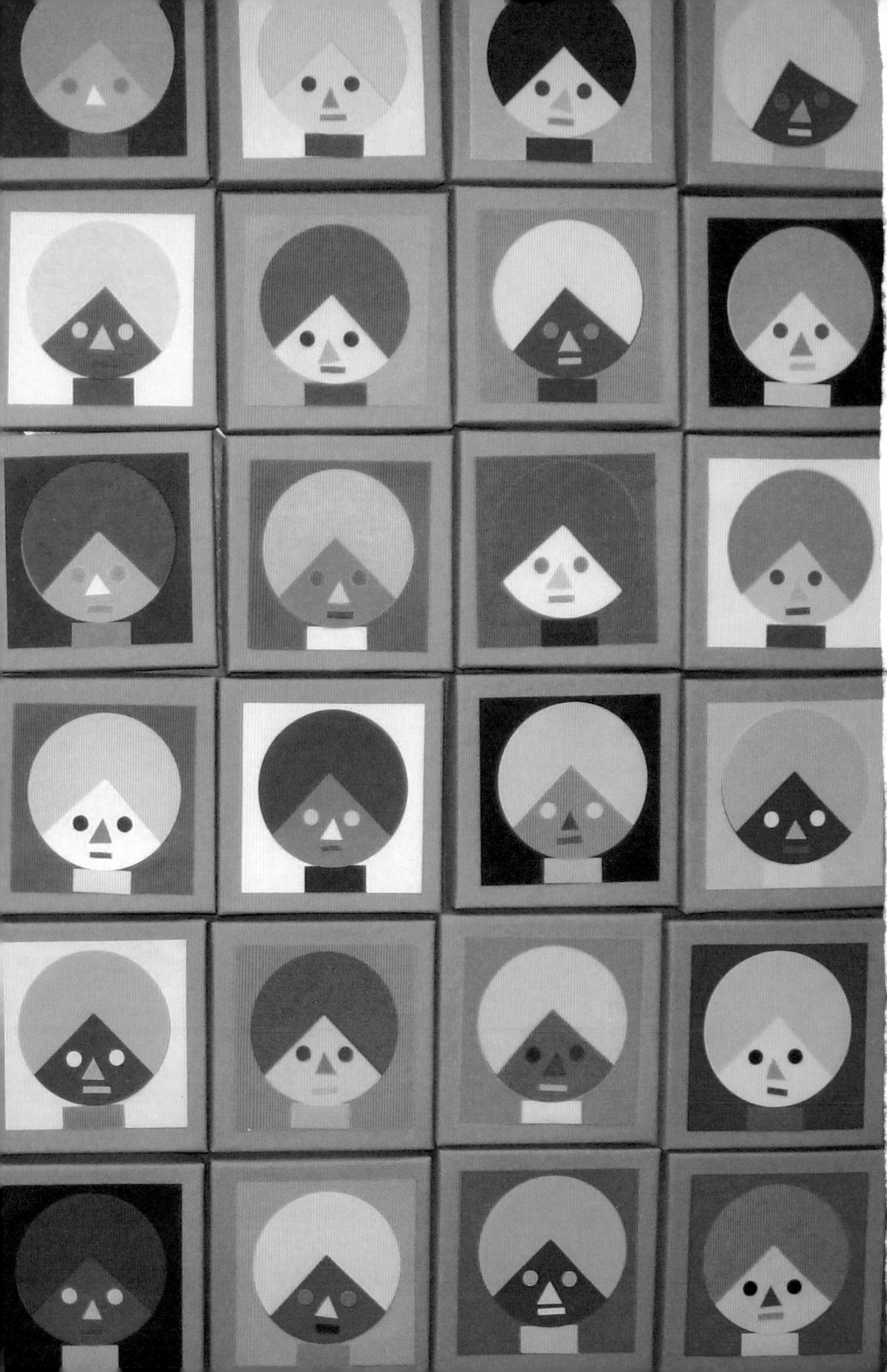

COMICS:
EASY AS ABC!

The *Essential Guide* to *Comics* for *Kids*

For kids, parents, teachers, and librarians!

FOR VISUAL READERS

TOON BOOKS®

NEW YORK

A JUNIOR LIBRARY GUILD SELECTION

Childhood drawing by Ivan Brunetti, age 6
(Brunetti grew up in Italy and was copying local Disney comics.)

Editorial Director, Editor, & Book Design: FRANÇOISE MOULY
IVAN BRUNETTI'S artwork was drawn with pencil and India Ink on Bristol board and colored digitally.

FOR VISUAL READERS

TOON GRAPHICS

A TOON Graphic™ © 2019 individual contributors & TOON Books, an imprint of RAW Junior, LLC, 27 Greene Street, New York, NY 10013.
TOON Books® and TOON Graphics™ are trademarks of RAW Junior, LLC. All rights reserved. No part of this book may be used or reproduced in any manner whatsoever without written permission except in the case of brief quotations embodied in critical articles and reviews.
Library of Congress Cataloging-in-Publication Data: Names: Brunetti, Ivan, author. | Mouly, Françoise, editor. Title: Comics : easy as ABC! : looking at comics for parents, teachers, and librarians : making comics for kids, kindergarten and up / Ivan Brunetti ; Françoise Mouly, editor. Description: New York, NY : TOON Books, [2019] | Includes bibliographical references and index. Identifiers: LCCN 2018041483 | ISBN 978-1-943145-44-7 (hardcover : alk. paper) Subjects: LCSH: Comic books, strips, etc.--Technique. Classification: LCC NC1764 .B77 2019 | DDC 741.5/1--dc23 LC record available at https://lccn.loc.gov/2018041483. All our books are Smyth Sewn (the highest library-quality binding available) and printed with soy-based inks on acid-free, woodfree paper harvested from responsible sources. Printed in China by C&C Offset Printing Co., Ltd. Distributed to the trade by Consortium Book Sales & Distribution, a division of Ingram Content Group; orders (866) 400-5351; ips@ingramcontent.com; www.cbsd.com.
ISBN 978-1-943145-44-7 (hardcover)   ISBN 978-1-943145-39-3 (softcover)
19 20 21 22 23 24 C&C 10 9 8 7 6 5 4 3 2 1
WWW.TOON-BOOKS.COM

WHY THIS BOOK?

by Françoise Mouly

Many years ago, I fell in love. I fell in love with a cartoonist, and I fell in love with what he was so passionate about: comics. "Everything I know, I learned from comics," said art spiegelman. (This was Spiegelman all in lowercase, before he went on to be a famous cartoonist, the Pulitzer Prize-winning author of *Maus: A Survivor's Tale* – although as another cartoonist, Dan Clowes, pointed out, "Being a famous cartoonist is like being a famous badminton player.") But I digress. "Everything I know, I learned from comics: economics from *Uncle Scrooge* ... philosophy from *Peanuts* ... and feminism from *Little Lulu*. Ethics, aesthetics, and everything else from *MAD Magazine*." And so it was for me.

I have spent a lifetime editing and publishing cartoonists. (Besides TOON Books, which I founded ten years ago, I've been the art editor of *The New Yorker* for more than twenty-five years.) And how do you edit cartoons and comics? If nothing else, this book will show you how much thought and skill go into effective visual communication. You'll get an inkling of the discussions I've had over the years about whether this character should face left or right, or about how to find just the right facial expression or the right color to support the overall idea. In advocating for comics for kids, in speaking with teachers, librarians, and parents, I've realized how little common vocabulary we have to understand and appreciate what goes into minting comics. (Speaking of vocabulary, see the index on page 49. You're about to be let in on many of the secrets of the trade by master cartoonist and teacher Ivan Brunetti. Once you finish the book, doodle away and you'll be able to express your delight using emanata–bursts and tears!)

Part of the attraction of the medium, especially for kids, is how fluidly comics are read. They are multisensory: when a story is well told, the reader is deeply engaged, mind, body and soul, in the magical world penned by the cartoonist. Yet even if Charles Schulz's *Peanuts* or Bill Watterson's *Calvin and Hobbes* are literally "easy to read," their power comes from the fact that the artists have distilled universal truths into clear, specific, and often deeply funny short stories–not easy to do day after day. As James Sturm (a cartoonist who also founded and runs a comics school) has said, comics are not just words and pictures–they are more akin to poetry and graphic design. So if this book makes you fall in love with comics as I did, head over heels, as both a reader and a fan, it will have accomplished its purpose. Beyond that, if it encourages more budding cartoonists and opens a path to the future for them, I'll be delighted. I'll leave the last word to Liniers, one of the very few cartoonists who, these days, still manages the astonishing feat of producing a new strip, *Macanudo*, every single day: "Oh, Ivan Brunetti, where was this book when I was a kid and wanted to become a cartoonist!?" Liniers asked us. "You lucky, lucky 21st-century kids!"

KIDS: BE A CARTOONIST!

Comics are made by people with just a pen on paper. Look at comics you like and copy them. The more you draw, the better you'll become. There is not one right way to draw—the fun is finding your own way of drawing.

DOODLE!

Doodling is the first step in cartooning. Let your pen run on paper, and just enjoy making simple shapes. Your doodles will become simpler at each step. When we have no time to think about the drawing, we get closer to the idea of the thing being drawn.

USEFUL TOOLS

The only tools you need are:

> Paper
> Pencil
> Life

Get a lot of scrap paper. (We don't recommend doodling all over your homework or in this book!) Try various pens and pencils, and choose a pen you enjoy making marks with. If things don't work out, crumple the paper and aim it at the wastebasket.

TRY IT!

DRAW A CIRCLE. THEN DRAW IT AGAIN AND AGAIN AS FAST AS POSSIBLE.

BASIC SHAPES

DOODLE! Draw these shapes freehand and get comfortable making your versions of circles, squares, and triangles.

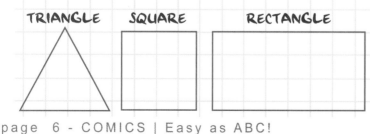

TRIANGLE   SQUARE   RECTANGLE

CIRCLES

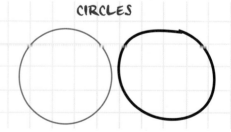

FAMOUS CARTOONIST QUOTE:
"Style is the difference between a circle and the way you draw it."
—Pablo Picasso

MAKE YOUR MARKS!

Make a few straight, bold lines. Then draw many lines together.

Make curved lines. Then draw many curved lines together.

Fill a piece of paper with dots. Doodle by connecting the dots with straight and curved lines.

PATTERNS!
Have fun making patterns with lines, dots, or squiggles. Simple patterns can help with clothes and costumes.

WHAT WORKS?

Cartoonists often find new ideas in their doodles.

SNAILS ARE FUN TO DRAW!
KEVIN McCLOSKEY MAKES A SNAIL OUT OF A "6"

6

Start with a 6.

Circle around a few times.

Close up the shell.

Draw the body and eyes.

Don't forget the mucus!

The trick with snails is to draw...

S-L-O-W-L-Y!

"IVAN BRUNETTI IS THE GREATEST TEACHER OF CARTOONING IN THE WHOLE WORLD... REALLY!"

~ *CHRIS WARE*, MIDDLE-AGED DAD AND WEEKLY DINING COMPANION OF MR. BRUNETTI,
AS WELL AS AUTHOR OF VARIOUS TOMES OF LIGHT PICTORIAL FICTION UNWORTHY OF MENTION

PRO TIP #66: GET A *PILLOW!*

FACES

Draw circles or ovals for the face. Place the eyes in the middle, but put them lower if you want your character to look younger.

PRO TIP #67:

DON'T FORGET TO *EXERCISE!*

"Whenever you want someone to stop talking, tell them that you absolutely must sketch their wonderful face. They will sit quiet and still for up to an hour, and you can doodle in peace."
–LEMONY SNICKET, AUTHOR OF *A SERIES OF UNFORTUNATE EVENTS*

With a few simple shapes, you can draw many different faces and expressions.

TRY IT!

MAKE FACES IN FRONT OF THE MIRROR!

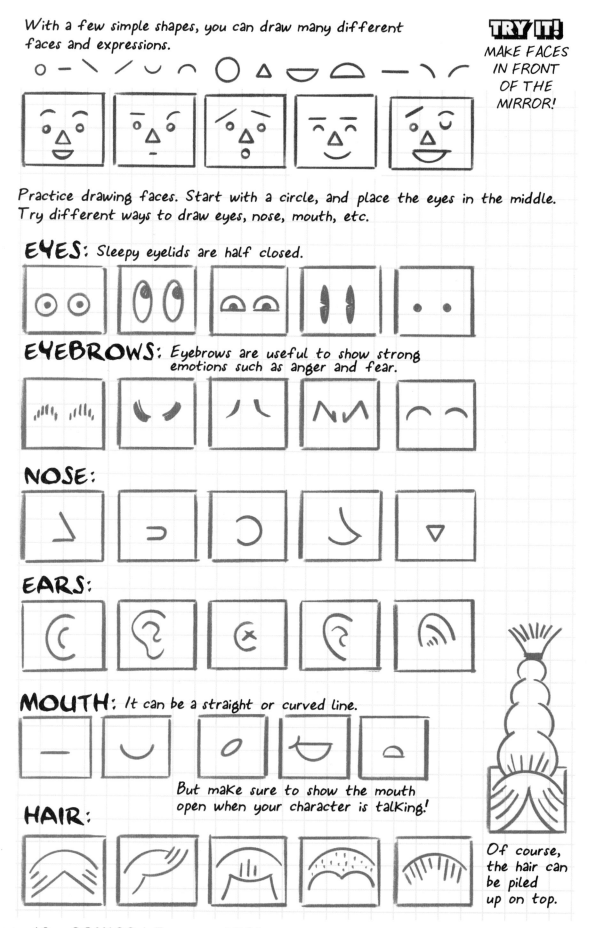

Practice drawing faces. Start with a circle, and place the eyes in the middle. Try different ways to draw eyes, nose, mouth, etc.

EYES: Sleepy eyelids are half closed.

EYEBROWS: Eyebrows are useful to show strong emotions such as anger and fear.

NOSE:

EARS:

MOUTH: It can be a straight or curved line.

But make sure to show the mouth open when your character is talking!

HAIR:

Of course, the hair can be piled up on top.

EMOTIONS

Give your characters different emotions by varying the eyebrows, the eyes, and the mouth.

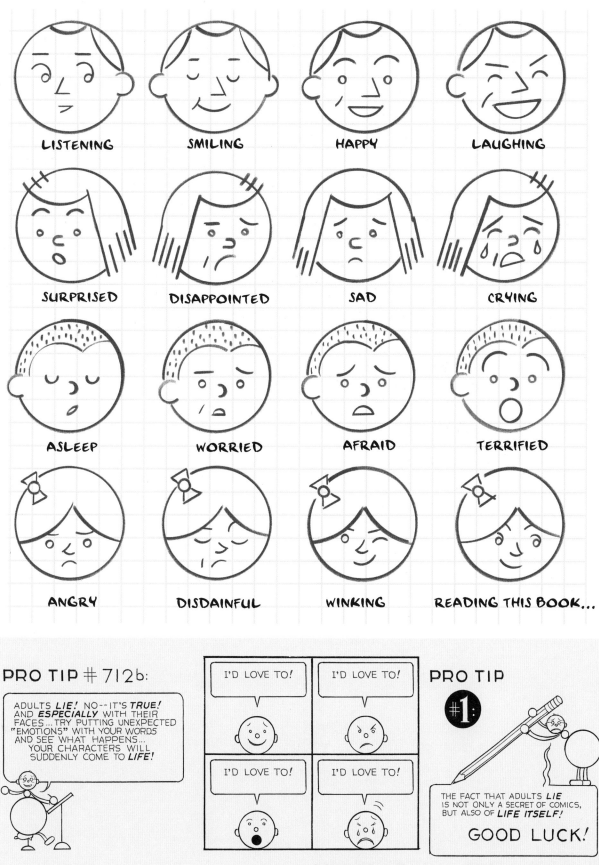

LISTENING   SMILING   HAPPY   LAUGHING

SURPRISED   DISAPPOINTED   SAD   CRYING

ASLEEP   WORRIED   AFRAID   TERRIFIED

ANGRY   DISDAINFUL   WINKING   READING THIS BOOK...

PRO TIP # 712b:

ADULTS *LIE!* NO--IT'S *TRUE!* AND *ESPECIALLY* WITH THEIR FACES...TRY PUTTING UNEXPECTED "EMOTIONS" WITH YOUR WORDS AND SEE WHAT HAPPENS... YOUR CHARACTERS WILL SUDDENLY COME TO *LIFE!*

I'D LOVE TO!

I'D LOVE TO!

I'D LOVE TO!

I'D LOVE TO!

PRO TIP

#1:

THE FACT THAT ADULTS *LIE* IS NOT ONLY A SECRET OF COMICS, BUT ALSO OF *LIFE ITSELF!*

GOOD LUCK!

PROFILES

TRY DIFFERENT NOSES, EYES, EARS...

  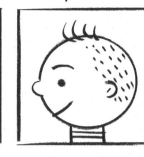 

WHAT WORKS?
JUST DOODLE, AND YOU'LL FIND NEW CHARACTERS AND EMOTIONS.

AND EMOTIONS!

LAUGHTER: the mouth opens, the eyes close, and the head tilts up.

ANGER: the eyebrows turn down, and the mouth and nose go up. Showing teeth is a sign of extreme anger.

GRIEF: the mouth turns down, the eyes close, and tears appear.

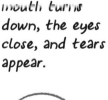 

SURPRISE: the eyebrows rise, and the eyes and mouth open wide.

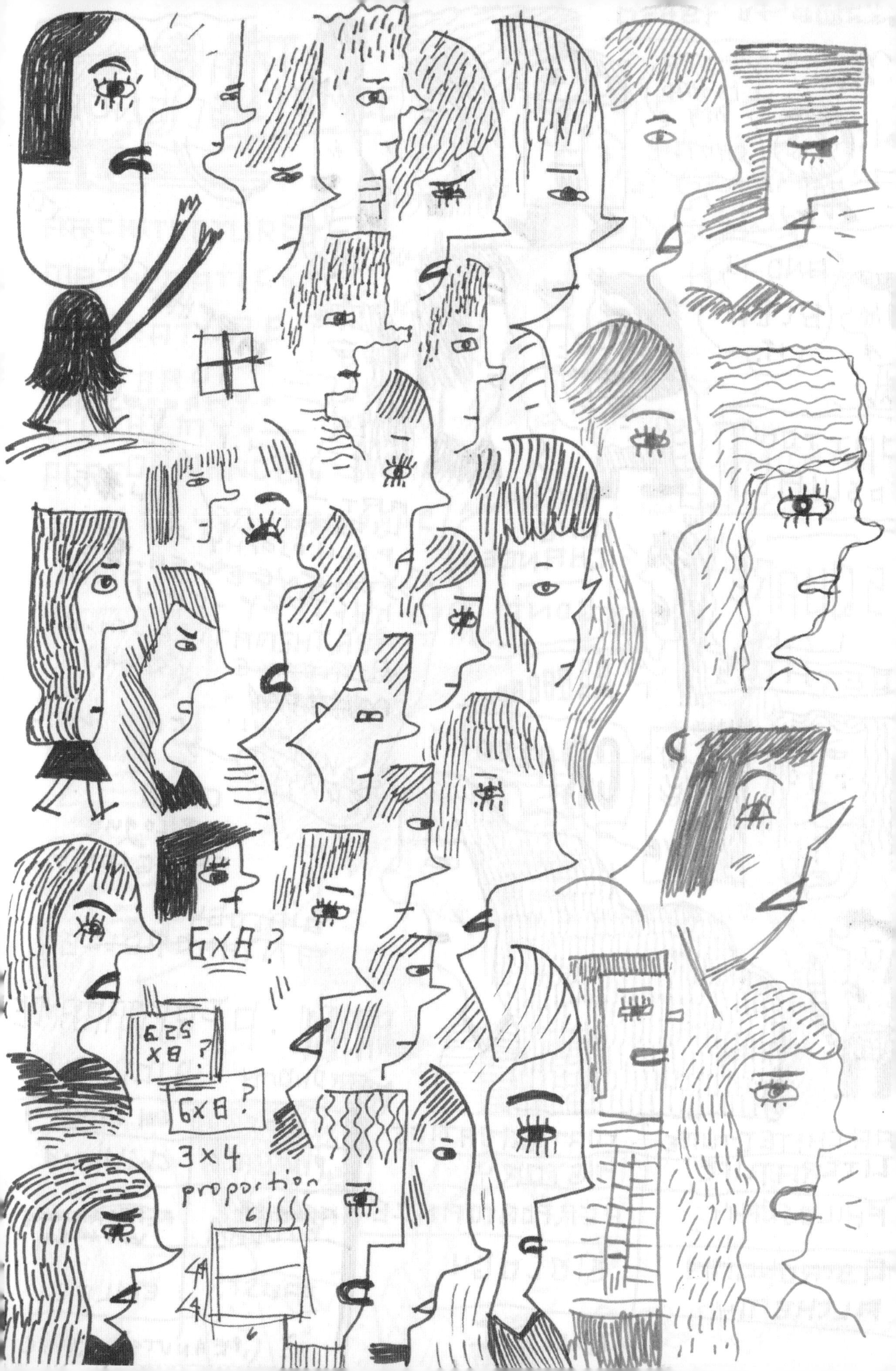
6x8?
6x8?
3x4
proportion

ABCs COME TO PLAY:

Use the alphabet to doodle new characters. In the alphabet and in numbers, you'll find your basic shapes. Use them as noses, hats, or legs.

You can use different color pens—as I did here—or the same pen.

CHARACTERS

MAKE EACH CHARACTER SPECIAL!

Clothes and props help us
define our characters.

Make this young woman
special: give her a lovely
mustache!

GIVE EVERY
CHARACTER
SOMETHING
UNIQUE: A
PATTERNED
SHIRT, GLASSES,
OR CURLY HAIR --
SO THEY ARE EASY
TO RECOGNIZE.

BODIES

Drawing stick people is a fun and simple way to get
started creating characters and telling stories. But
stick people aren't as easy as they look.

Sometimes the lines
don't connect, or it can
be difficult to get the
proportions right.

The stick arm and legs are useful, so let's hold on to those. Using a circle for a head also works well, so let's keep that idea. But what if we used a simple shape, like a square, for the body? That gives the head something solid to rest on.

MIX AND MATCH

You don't have to use just squares, rectangles, or circles. Other SIMPLE shapes: triangles, ovals, and more work well too.

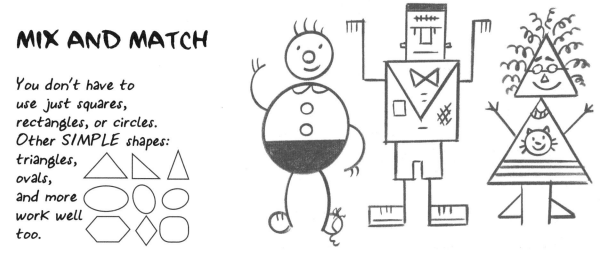

TRY DIFFERENT BODIES

BODY LANGUAGE
MAKE YOUR CHARACTER MOVE

If we can bend and twist our stick arms, making them a little rounder, we can add a little depth and some movement to our characters, giving them a sense of life on the paper.

You can always "flesh out" the stick person.

DRAW YOUR OWN!

Remember to start with simple shapes.

I'm upside-down

Let the body show us, instead of telling us in words

Don't just show "TALKING HEADS." You'll miss an opportunity to show what the body can tell us about the characters.

PERSONALITIES:
What people do tells us about their personalities.

bold

careless

cautious

just watching

afraid

hot dog!

ANIMALS

Animals are fun to draw. Use simple shapes for them as well.

"If your drawing of an animal does not turn out the way you like, remember that the animal probably wouldn't draw you very well, either."

–LEMONY SNICKET,
AUTHOR OF *A SERIES OF UNFORTUNATE EVENTS*

Look at real animals and draw them: it will fuel your imagination!

MORE ANIMALS!

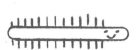

KEVIN McCLOSKEY,
AUTHOR OF
WE DIG WORMS!, **SAYS:**
"The best comics are not just characters standing stiffly, talking back and forth. Comics can do more. Zoom in on the eyes to show expression. Zoom out and show we're on Mars! Use your imagination!"

You can trace coins and glasses for circles and use rulers for straight lines.

A DAY IN A CAT'S LIFE

SLEEPING

STRETCHING

WALKING

REACHING

SPILLING

EATING AND DRINKING

STARTLED

RUNNING

PEEKING

WALKING BACK

YAWNING

SLEEPING

COMICS LANGUAGE
USEFUL TOOLS FOR CARTOONISTS

Use lines to show movement.

motion lines

action lines

Cartoonists can use symbols.

ZZZZ

Speed lines make anything go faster.

Use lines to show texture and surfaces.

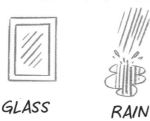

GLASS RAIN FUZZY

Stars will make something look shiny.

EMANATA: Named by cartoonist Mort Walker, the lines, bursts, and squiggles that indicate emotion or heat from the sun often come in handy.

SURPRISE HEAT ANGER

Tears can also mean surprise and sweat.

SURPRISE

SWEAT

And tears can be tears.

Here's a story told with emanata, bursts, and big tears.

HEROES OR VILLAINS

MAKE YOUR CHARACTER CUTE:

Place the eyes, nose, and mouth low in the face for that cute look.

freckles
smile

MAKE YOUR CHARACTER MENACING:

For bad guys, use what you learned about eyebrows...

...and sweat marks!

A small head on a big body.

A furrowed brow shows ill intentions.

Hands that will grab!

Show some teeth!

Monsters cast shadows!

PROPS

Props are the objects that help you set the scene-just like in the theater.

Draw everything you see around you, to understand it better. Then use your notes, your imagination — and your memory!

SCALE & SETTING

A human figure is usually 5 1/2 heads tall. But in comics, you can play with the scale and give your characters big or small heads.

Children have much bigger heads relative to their bodies than adults. That's why a character with a big head (and big baby eyes) looks "cute."

USE CONTRAST IN SCALE →

Kid   baby

tall player   short referee

big monster

small buildings

mother   child

You can establish setting with few details:

Where are we?

We're in a car, in the city.

Leaving the city.

Enjoying the beautiful view.

PERSPECTIVE

TIPS FROM **SERGIO GARCÍA SÁNCHEZ,** CO-AUTHOR WITH NADJA SPIEGELMAN OF *LOST IN NYC, A SUBWAY ADVENTURE.*

FOREGROUND AND BACKGROUND

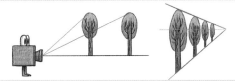

We see objects in front of us as much bigger than those that are far away.

Draw what's in front first, then what's in the back. The background needs few details.

PERSPECTIVE

Seen froim below.

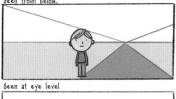

Seen at eye level

Seen from above.

Perspective drawing shows how things appear from the point of view of someone looking. The scene changes depending on where you place the horizon line.

To create the illusion of depth on paper, artists have developed a set of rules called perspective. Now, 3D games and software use the same rules to create the appearance of 3-dimensional space.

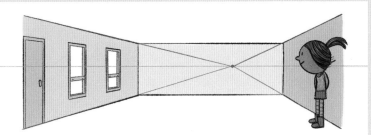

ONE-POINT PERSPECTIVE can be useful to show the inside of a room.

TWO-POINT perspective is often used to show buildings from the outside.

PERSPECTIVE AND COMICS

With comics, you need to show only enough of the setting for the reader to understand where the story takes place. There are many ways to do this.

1. Show your characters next to and above each other.

2. Use two-point perspective. Figures in the background will be smaller.

3. Cartoonist Ivan Brunetti came up with his own way of representing space.

In the first panel of Brunetti's _Wordplay_, we see Anne-Marie and her friends lined up in a classroom. The artist's decision to keep the lines of the tables parallel makes this "long shot" easy to read.

Who can tell us what a compound word is?

POINT OF VIEW

Depending on where you place the point of view (called the eye level,) a scene can be seen from below (worm's eye) or above (bird's eye.)

WORM'S EYE

BIRD'S EYE

ANOTHER BIRD'S EYE

LONG SHOT - MEDIUM SHOT - CLOSE-UP

A long shot (left) sets the scene. Close-ups (above) are a good way to bring attention to the character's emotions.

After the long shot, much of the comics story can be told with "medium shots," as in this next page of _Wordplay_. The cartoonist no longer needs to show the whole scene.

Two words that join to make a new word?

YES, Annemarie!

Like homework?

Good!

BALLOONS & LETTERING

Balloons tell us what the character says or thinks.

Make sure to follow these RULES for the balloons:

Place the balloons first, to make sure they'll fit.

The SHAPE of the balloon and the size of the lettering tell us HOW to read the words.

LETTERING

When it comes to lettering...

STYLE can tell us about the character.

SPLASH PAGE

The first page of the story (the "SPLASH") has the title and puts us right in the middle of the action.

TITLE LETTERING

Cartoonists often use block letters to make the title stand out.

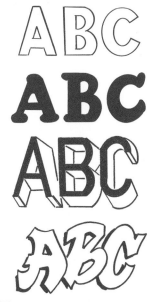

Trace the outline of your letters. Fill them in or draw a shadow on one side.

PAY SPECIAL ATTENTION TO THE LETTERING OF THE

TITLE

CAPTION BOX means that some-one is telling us the story...

ROAR

WHOOSH

CRANK CRANK

SPLASH!

Mmmm

SOUND EFFECTS (also called onomatopoeia)
are best when the word styles can match the sound.

PAGE & PANELS

PUNCH LINE

NOTE: it's good if your last panel can become a "PUNCH LINE," a joke that recaps and ends the whole story.

COMICS VOCABULARY:

Explained on this spread: panels, panel borders, gutter, silent panel, timing, panel sizes, spread, punch line.

"Cartooning is about finding a rhythm."

–JAMES STURM,
CO-AUTHOR OF
ADVENTURES IN CARTOONING

BY ALEC LONGSTRETH

Tall scenes need tall panels.

Wide scenes need wide panels.

SIMPLER IS BETTER

Give your characters enough room to breathe.

Two facing pages are called a SPREAD and can be used to dramatic effect.

TELL YOUR STORY!

When searching for ideas, think about what you want to draw.
Choosing a setting sometimes helps you think of a story.

WHICH COMES FIRST: WRITING OR DRAWING?

You can start with either, but think about what you'll be drawing.
Try to show the characters somewhere, doing something.

It's always good to let pictures suggest other pictures and tell the story.

NEW YORKER CARTOONIST **ROZ CHAST**'s TOON TALK

For me, a cartoon starts with an idea...

Something that makes me laugh...

Heh, heh

BABY POTATOES IN WATER

... or weirds me out...

Ew

BABY POTATOES IN WATER

OR BOTH!

It's like telling someone a little story. You want to tell it clearly and to not be too blabby.

Sometimes I'm a little blabby.

Oh, well.

Don't worry about making mistakes. Most of what I do winds up in the garbage. No one needs to know.

R. Chst

NEIL GAIMAN,

AUTHOR OF *SANDMAN* AND MANY OTHER BOOKS AND COMICS, SAYS:

"Comics taught me how to read pictures, how to read for context, how to spell strange and unfamiliar words. They opened my eyes to different worlds and different ways of seeing the world. They made me think, and they made me dream.

So when I grew up, I made comics, too. And I learned that comics are as much fun to make as they are to read. But it takes much longer to make them than it does to read them ..."

PROMPTS

Choose some prompts from those below (by Ivan Brunetti) or the facing page (by Renée French), or create your own. Then make up a story!

FIRST CHARACTER:

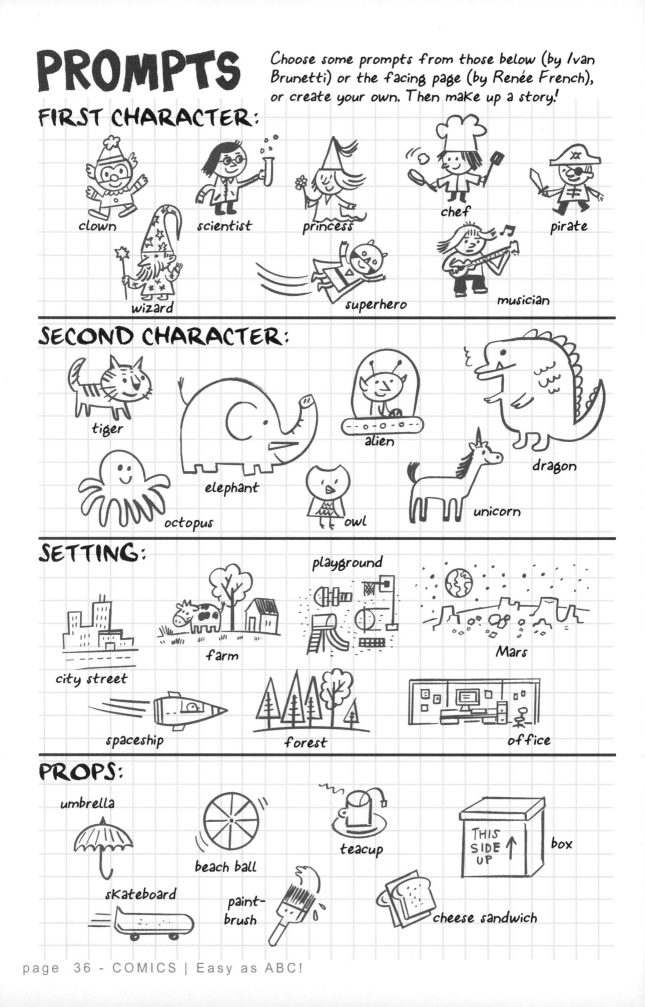

clown

scientist

princess

chef

pirate

wizard

superhero

musician

SECOND CHARACTER:

tiger

elephant

alien

dragon

octopus

owl

unicorn

SETTING:

playground

city street

farm

Mars

spaceship

forest

office

PROPS:

umbrella

beach ball

teacup

box

skateboard

paint-brush

cheese sandwich

MORE PROMPTS:

"Look into your character's eyes. She or he will tell you the story."

RENÉE FRENCH,
AUTHOR OF
BARRY'S BEST BUDDY

FIRST CHARACTER:

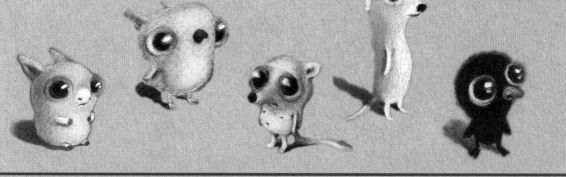

SECOND CHARACTER:

SETTING:

PROPS:

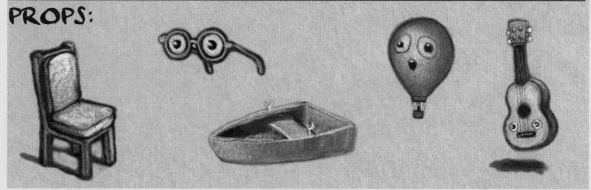

SHORT STRIPS

Here are a few four-panel strips by various artists, from the 4PANEL Project website [**http://4panel.ca/**], an online gathering of artists who like to post short strips. For Mark Laliberte, who started the website, telling a story in only four panels is challenging and inspiring. It doesn't take a lot of space to develop distinct characters, and having limited space encourages artists to communicate the essence of their idea efficiently.

> *"Create a four-panel comic. It can be autobiographical, experimental, or a collection of facts about something that interests you. Find the right rhythm for your sequence. Think of the four-panel comic as the* haiku *of cartooning."*
>
> **–JAMES STURM, CO-AUTHOR OF *ADVENTURES IN CARTOONING***

MARK LALIBERTE *Turning the Lights Back On*

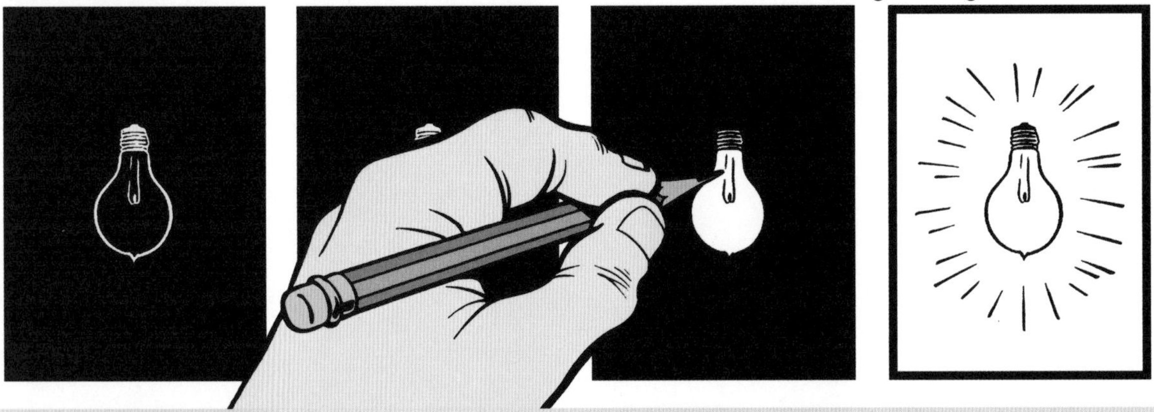

ALEX SCHUBERT *Little Buddies*

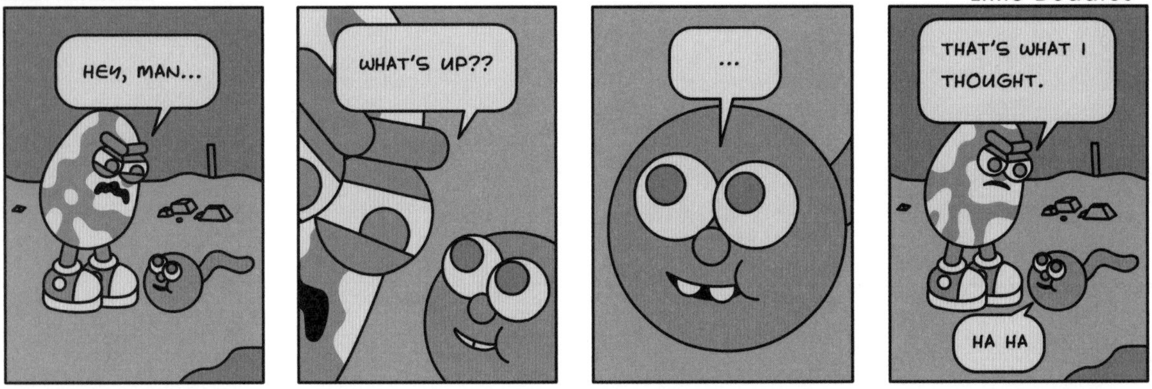
HEY, MAN...
WHAT'S UP??
...
THAT'S WHAT I THOUGHT.
HA HA

DAVIDE BART SALVEMINI *The Magician*

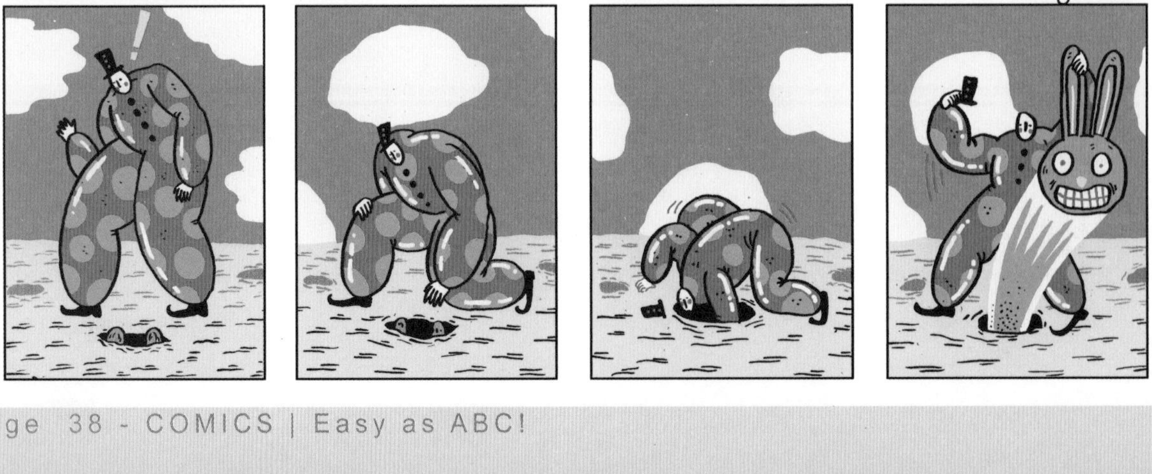

ERIK NEBEL — *Stormy Weather*

MARK CONNERY — *A Tragedy*

BRIAN ROPPEL — *Force of Habit*

AARON LINTON — *Found Object Comics*

DRAW YOUR OWN CONCLUSION:

by **ART SPIEGELMAN**, AUTHOR OF *MAUS: A SURVIVOR'S TALE*

THE END

FIND YOUR OWN VOICE:

"Find your own voice – don't just imitate other artists. Draw and think and draw and think. Don't avoid pain. Don't harden your heart. Feel those feelings, and draw them. Your voice will come out on its own. Then, when it comes out, trust it."

–ELEANOR DAVIS, AUTHOR OF *STINKY*

Monsters can have many different moods.

On the first page of her book, *Stinky*, **ELEANOR DAVIS** uses many details (a bird with a clothespin on its nose, flies buzzing around a toad, bats on the ceiling, a spider spinning its web, a bouquet of reeds from the swamp in a vinegar bottle, and many more) to give us information about her main character, a monster named Stinky.

PARENTS, TEACHERS, LIBRARIANS:
HOW TO READ COMICS WITH KIDS

Kids LOVE comics! The details in the pictures make them want to read the words. Comics beg for repeated readings and let both emerging and reluctant readers enjoy stories with a rich vocabulary. Here are a few tips for reading comics with kids...

① FIND THE RIGHT BOOK

There are many comics and graphic novels out there, but not all are appropriate for every age. Look for titles made especially for children. It's best to choose a story that fits the child's age and interests.

"Many times students who do not want to read or write black text on a white page will eagerly read TOON Books and create colorful illustrations and text of their own."

—Brian Wilhorn, reading teacher and author of HelpReadersLoveReading.com

WHAT WORKS?

The TOON Books collection, designed for emerging readers, also works wonders with reluctant readers.

② GUIDE YOUNG READERS

WHAT WORKS?

Keep your fingertip <u>below</u> the character who is speaking.

HAM IT UP!

Think of the comic book story as a play. Don't hesitate to be a ham! Read with expression and intonation. Assign parts or get kids to supply the sound effects— a great way to reinforce phonics skills.

LET THEM GUESS

Comics provide a great deal of context for the words, so emerging readers can make informed guesses. In *Benny and Penny in Just Pretend,* by Geoffrey Hayes, for example, the first time the word "pirate" is introduced, the artist also shows a pirate ship, two pirate hats, and two pirate flags.

5 TALK ABOUT THE PICTURES

The artist communicates information through the shape of the panels (and can make you laugh by putting panels upside down!). Readers will follow what the characters look at. Show young readers how the composition of the right-hand page below points to the bird flying away, breaking out of the panel.

WHAT WORKS?

Get kids talking, and you'll be surprised at how perceptive they are about pictures.

POINT OUT THAT EACH BOX IS CALLED A **PANEL** AND THAT EACH PANEL IS A UNIT OF TIME. ALSO HELP KIDS RECOGNIZE THE DIFFERENT BALLOONS:

SPEECH BALLOONS   THOUGHT BALLOONS   SOUND EFFECTS

6 TAKE TIME WITH SILENT PANELS

Comics use panels to mark time, and silent panels count. Look and "read" even when there are no words. Often, humor is all in the timing!

7 PICTURES TELL THE STORY!

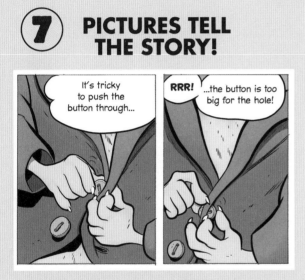

In a comic, you can often read the story even if you don't know all the words! Jeff Smith, the master cartoonist behind the *Bone* series and *Little Mouse Gets Ready*, is a visual storyteller. Get young readers to tell you what's happening in the sequence at right based on Little Mouse's facial expressions and body language.

WHAT WORKS?

When reading comics, kids see the hand of the artist, and it makes them want to tell their own stories. Encourage them to talk, write, and draw!

LET THEM REREAD   Not only do children love to read comics, they also love to REread them. When rereading a comic, kids find all the details that make comics so pleasurable, and when they reread, emerging readers become fluent readers.

9 ABOVE ALL, ENJOY!

There is, of course, never one right way to read, so go for the shared pleasure. Once children experience the pleasure of making the story happen in their heads, they have discovered the thrill of reading, and you won't be able to stop them. At that point, just go get them more books, and more comics.

THE TOON INTO READING™ PROGRAM

The award-winning TOON Books® are used extensively on school reading lists, in libraries, and at bedtime! Step by step, the TOON Books® will welcome your emerging or reluctant reader into a lifelong love of reading!

LEVEL 1 LEXILE BR-100 • GUIDED READING A-G • READING RECOVERY 7-10
GRADES K-1

FIRST COMICS FOR BRAND-NEW READERS

- 200–300 easy sight words
- short sentences
- often one character
- single time frame or theme
- 1–2 panels per page

LEVEL 2 LEXILE BR-170 • GUIDED READING G-J • READING RECOVERY 11-17
GRADES 1-2

EASY-TO-READ COMICS FOR EMERGING READERS

- 300–600 words
- short sentences and repetition
- story arc with few characters in a small world
- 1–4 panels per page

LEVEL 3 LEXILE 150-300 • GUIDED READING J-N • READING RECOVERY 17-19
GRADES 2-3

CHAPTER-BOOK COMICS FOR ADVANCED BEGINNERS

- 800–1000+ words in long sentences
- broad world as well as shifts in time and place
- long story divided into chapters
- reader needs to speculate and make connections

TOON-BOOKS.com

GET OUT THE CRAYONS!

Hey, kids! Copy this page and add colors to Benny and Penny's world. You can also cut out the panels and scramble them. Can you put them back in the correct order?

WHAT WORKS?

Read LOTS of comics, and when you reread them, pay attention to the choices the author made.

It's OK to copy and trace: all cartoonists learn that way.

WHAT WORKS?

Mr. Peach

OR THE JOYS OF TEACHING COMICS TO COLLEGE STUDENTS

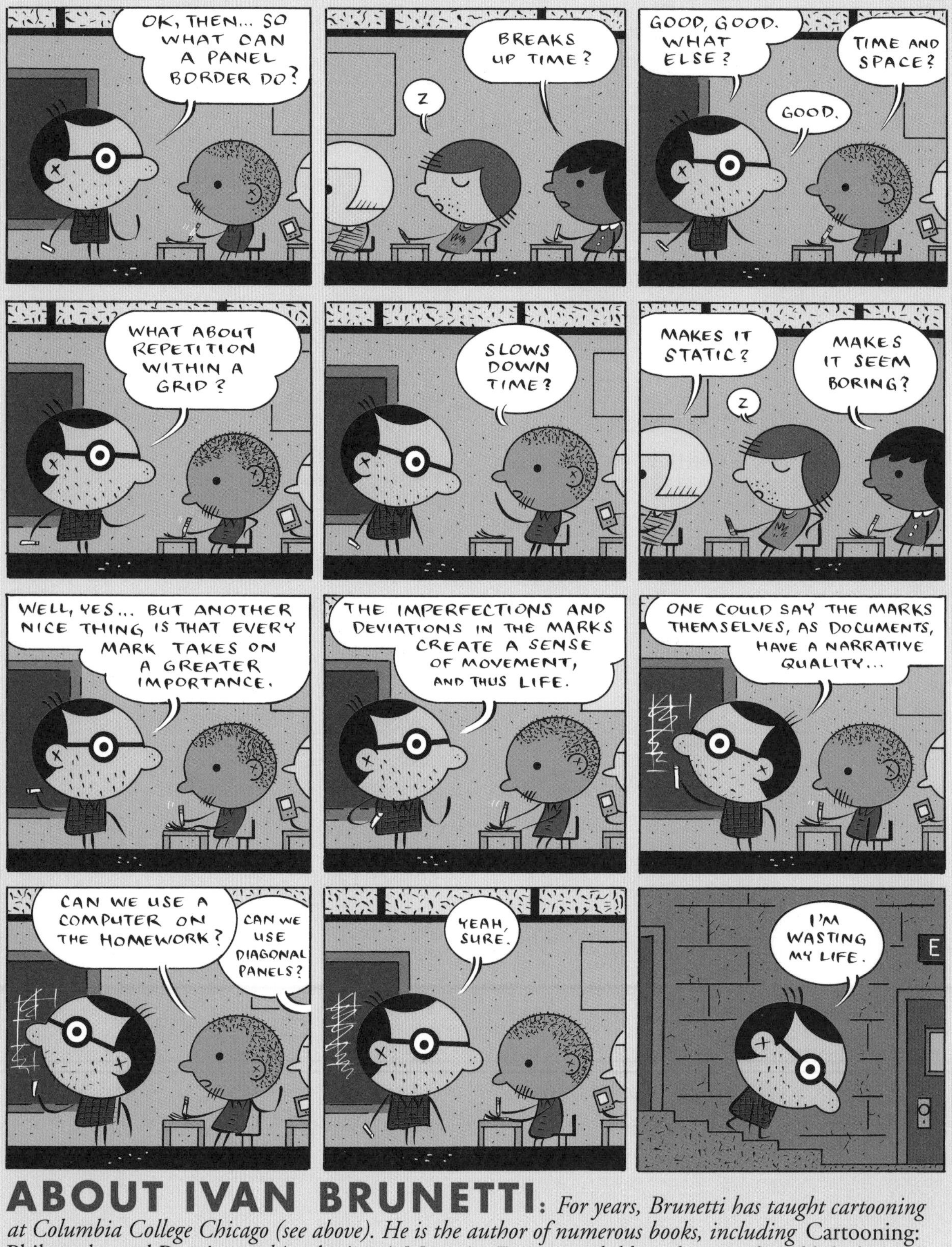

OK, THEN... SO WHAT CAN A PANEL BORDER DO?
Z
BREAKS UP TIME?
GOOD, GOOD. WHAT ELSE?
TIME AND SPACE?
GOOD.
WHAT ABOUT REPETITION WITHIN A GRID?
SLOWS DOWN TIME?
MAKES IT STATIC?
Z
MAKES IT SEEM BORING?
WELL, YES... BUT ANOTHER NICE THING IS THAT EVERY MARK TAKES ON A GREATER IMPORTANCE.
THE IMPERFECTIONS AND DEVIATIONS IN THE MARKS CREATE A SENSE OF MOVEMENT, AND THUS LIFE.
ONE COULD SAY THE MARKS THEMSELVES, AS DOCUMENTS, HAVE A NARRATIVE QUALITY...
CAN WE USE A COMPUTER ON THE HOMEWORK?
CAN WE USE DIAGONAL PANELS?
YEAH, SURE.
I'M WASTING MY LIFE.
E

ABOUT IVAN BRUNETTI: *For years, Brunetti has taught cartooning at Columbia College Chicago (see above). He is the author of numerous books, including* Cartooning: Philosophy and Practice *and* Aesthetics: A Memoir. *For young children, he recently published two hugely successful Level One TOON Books:* Wordplay *(2017) and* 3x4 *(2018).*

ABOUT THE CONTRIBUTORS

ROZ CHAST *is a cartoonist for* The New Yorker *and the author of many books for children.*

ELEANOR DAVIS's *first book,* Stinky, *was the recipient of a Geisel Award Honor.*

RENÉE FRENCH, *a cartoonist, created the Go gopher, the mascot of the Go programming language.*

NEIL GAIMAN *is the best-selling author of books and comics, many of which have been turned into movies and TV shows.*

ELISE GRAVEL *is a Canadian cartoonist and the author of many books for children.*

GEOFFREY HAYES, *who passed away in 2017, is the author of the Benny & Penny TOON books.*

LINIERS's *daily strip,* Macanudo, *is now syndicated in newspapers across the U.S.*

KEVIN McCLOSKEY *is the author of the hugely popular* Giggle and Learn *series.*

FRANÇOISE MOULY, *the art editor of* The New Yorker, *founded TOON Books ten years ago.*

SERGIO GARCÍA SÁNCHEZ *is a Spanish cartoonist who teaches at European universities.*

JEFF SMITH *is the author of the beloved* Bone *comics series.*

LEMONY SNICKET *is a writer and the author of the best-selling* A Series of Unfortunate Events.

ART SPIEGELMAN *is the Pulitzer Prize-winning author of* Maus: A Survivor's Tale.

JAMES STURM *is the director of Vermont's Center for Cartoon Studies as well a cartoonist.*

CHRIS WARE *is an award-winning cartoonist. He often gets together with his friend Ivan Brunetti to discuss comics.*

COMICS INDEX

DID YOU GET IT ALL? *Cartoonists have their own language, which is fun to learn and use. Here are some of the words and concepts discussed in this book, as well as the pages on which they appear.*

FURTHER RESOURCES

NOTE: While there's no substitute for unfettered access to books, comics, and an unlimited supply of scrap paper and pens, online resources can be a great support – hence this short list.

For younger kids

WWW.TOON-BOOKS.COM

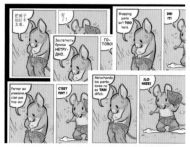

The TOON Books website (TOON Books is the publisher of this book) offers a wide array of free online resources:

• LESSON PLANS: Common Core guides–with an emphasis on developing students' visual literacy–are available for every TOON book. They include lesson plans, student activity sheets, and topics for the ELA Common Core Standards.

• PROFESSOR GARFIELD'S TOON BOOK READER: a nonprofit educational collaboration between Garfield the Cat and Ball State University, this resource allows children to read selected TOON Books online ... and in multiple languages: English, French, Spanish, Russian, and Chinese. An excellent resource in the classroom for ESL and ELL students. "Read-along videos" are available on the TOON Books YouTube channel.

• PROFESSOR GARFIELD'S CARTOON MAKER: Create your own one-panel cartoon. Just click and choose from backgrounds, characters, props, balloons, and text, and then save your completed work! Includes a 3-panel framework for short strips.

For older kids and grown-ups

HTTPS://WWW.CARTOONSTUDIES.ORG/PROGRAMS/CCS-ONE-WEEK-CARTOONING-WORKOUT/
A free one-week cartooning workout course designed by Alec Longstreth and James Sturm for Vermont's Center for Cartoon Studies. This seven-day email course is designed for aspiring cartoonists or those who need to get back into a creative groove.

HTTP://THENEARSIGHTEDMONKEY.TUMBLR.COM/ You can follow cartoonist and educator Lynda Barry's class at the University of Wisconsin's Institute for Discovery online, as Barry posts assignments and students' work on her tumblr.

SELECTED BIBLIOGRAPHY

For younger kids

NOTE: Some of the older books here, such as those by Ed Emberley or Syd Hoff, may be hard to find in print, but they're timeless classics worth searching for.

———

Books by Ed Emberley: Ed Emberley's Drawing Book of Faces, Drawing Book of Animals, Drawing Book of Trucks and Trains, Big Orange Drawing Book, and many more. Little, Brown Books for Young Readers. Using simple shapes, these are classics that will get would-be artists to draw just about anything and enjoy it.

———

Books by Syd Hoff: Drawing With Letters and Numbers, and many others. Stravon, Scholastic. Perfect for primary grades, when kids enjoy drawing pictures with letters.

———

James Sturm, Andrew Arnold, and Alexis Frederick-Frost: Adventures in Cartooning: How to Turn Your Doodles Into Comics, and many others in the series. First Second. This how-to-make-comics book doubles as a story about a knight on a quest and a magic elf.

The whole series is being reissued in 2019.

———

Raina Telgemeier: Share Your Smile: Raina's Guide to Telling Your Own Story, Scholastic. The best-selling author offers insight on her own comics-making and gives guidance on how to brainstorm ideas and use one's imagination to create stories.

———

Art Spiegelman & Françoise Mouly (editors): The Toon Treasury of Classic Children's Comics, Abrams Comicarts. The greatest stories for children culled from the golden age of comic books. Works by Carl Barks, John Stanley, Sheldon Mayer, among many, many others.

For older kids and grown-ups

Books by Jack Hamm, including Cartooning the Head and Figure, TarcherPerigee. The practical advice, thousands of step-by-step diagrams, and illustrations make this encyclopedia of cartoon techniques an essential reference for any artist's library.

———

Ivan Brunetti: Cartooning: Philosophy and Practice, Yale University Press. A clear, concise, and accessible book for all interested

in cartooning. With helpful insights and sequences of exercises, readers are encouraged to develop their own styles.

———

Books by Lynda Barry: What It Is and Syllabus: Notes from an Accidental Professor, Drawn & Quarterly. Inspirational guidebooks about how and why to be creative.

———

Books by Scott McCloud: Understanding Comics: The Invisible Art and Making Comics: Storytelling Secrets of Comics, Manga, and Graphic Novels, and more. Harper. Cartoonist and theorist Scott McCloud explores formal aspects of comics, outlining the fundamental vocabulary of the medium.

———

Jessica Abel & Matt Madden: Drawing Words and Writing Pictures, First Second. Designed as the textbook for a multiweek college comics course.

———

Mark Todd & Esther P. Watson: Whatcha Mean, What's a Zine? : The Art of Making Zines and Minicomics, HMH Books for Young Readers. How to design and print your own zine, so you can put it in others' hands. Teens will enjoy the subculture's indie spirit.

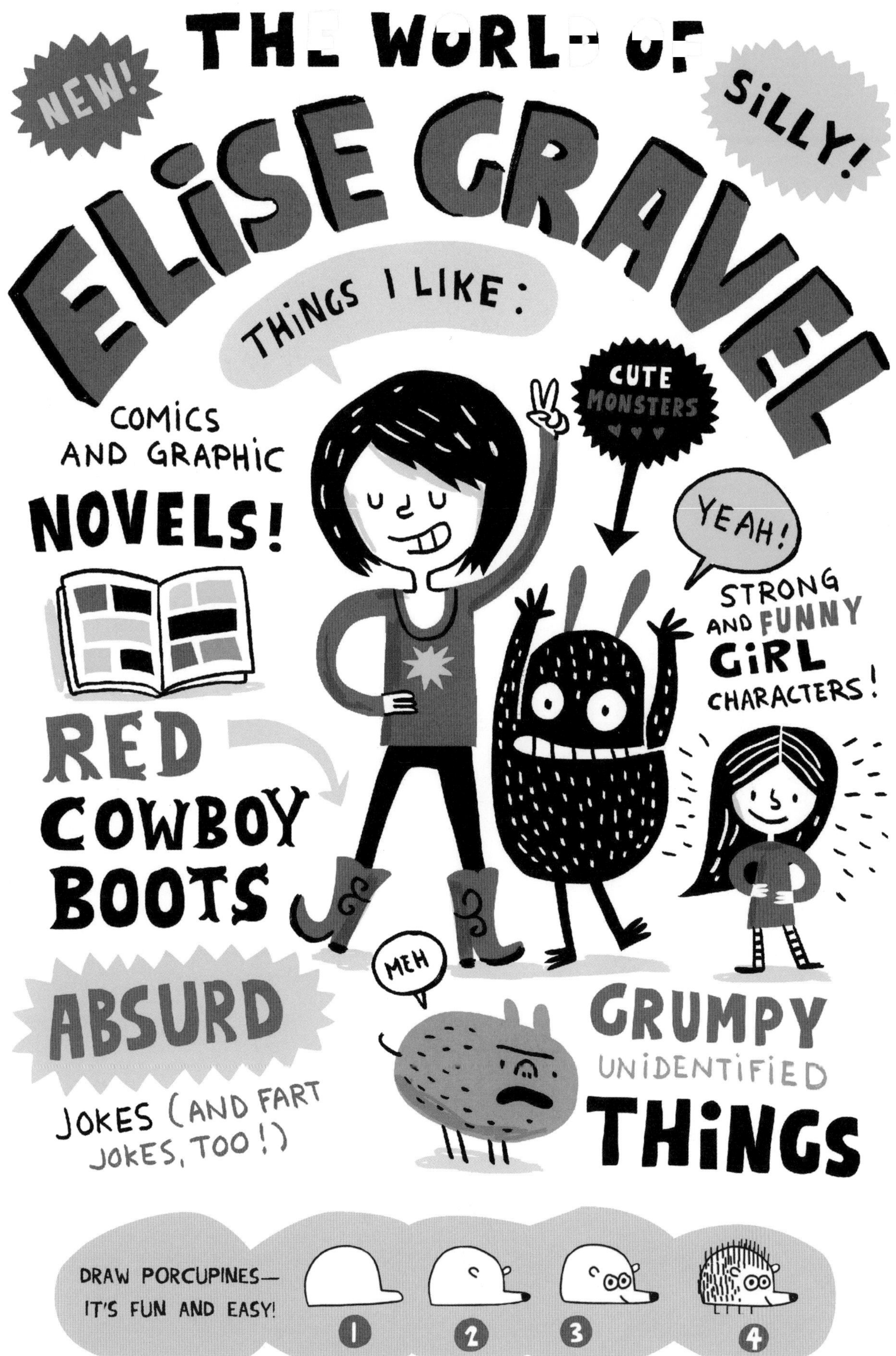
THE WORLD OF
NEW!
SILLY!
ELISE GRAVEL
THINGS I LIKE:
CUTE MONSTERS
COMICS AND GRAPHIC NOVELS!
YEAH!
STRONG AND FUNNY GIRL CHARACTERS!
RED COWBOY BOOTS
MEH
ABSURD JOKES (AND FART JOKES, TOO!)
GRUMPY UNIDENTIFIED THINGS
DRAW PORCUPINES— IT'S FUN AND EASY!
1
2
3
4

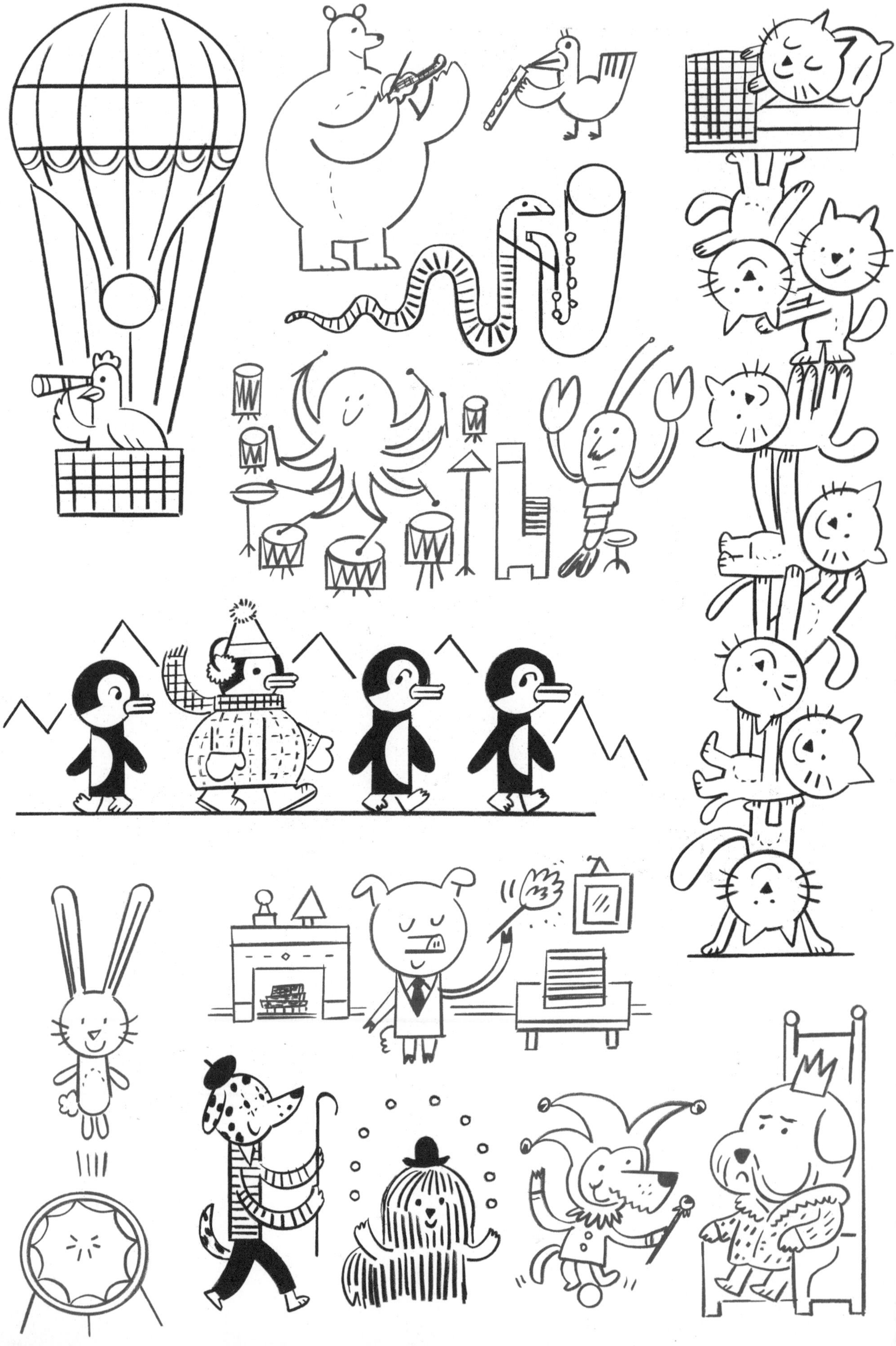